Great MOVIE MUSIC of the 20th CENTURY

ISBN 0-634-00987-7

HAL•LEONARD®
CORPORATION

7777 W. BLUEMOUND RD. P.O. BOX 13819 MILWAUKEE, WI 53213

Visit Hal Leonard Online at
www.halleonard.com

CONTENTS

ALMOST PARADISE

Love Theme from the Paramount Motion Picture FOOTLOOSE

Words by DEAN PITCHFORD
Music by ERIC CARMEN

(Male:) I thought that dreams be - longed to
(Male:) It seems like per - fect love's so

oth - er men, 'cause each time I got close they'd
hard to find. I'd al - most giv - en up. You

fall a - part a - gain. *(Female:)* I feared my heart would beat in
must have read my mind. *(Female:)* And all these dreams I saved for a

BABY, IT'S COLD OUTSIDE

from the Motion Picture NEPTUNE'S DAUGHTER

By FRANK LOESSER

BE OUR GUEST
from Walt Disney's BEAUTY AND THE BEAST

Lyrics by HOWARD ASHMAN
Music by ALAN MENKEN

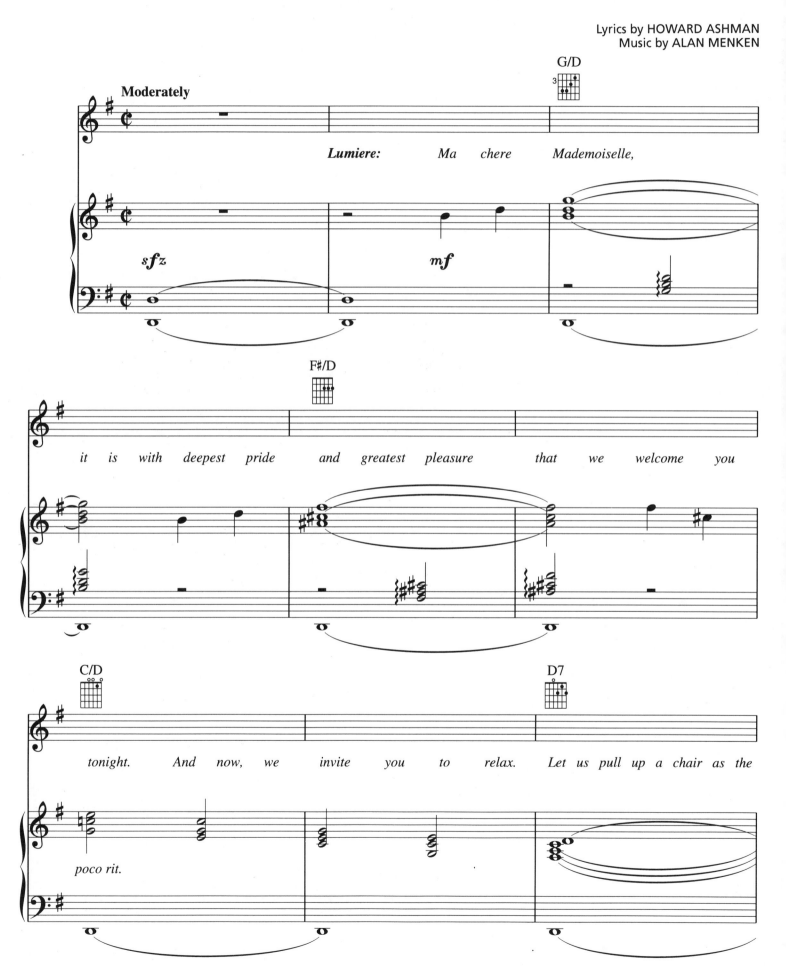

Lumiere: *Ma chere Mademoiselle,*

it is with deepest pride and greatest pleasure that we welcome you

tonight. And now, we invite you to relax. Let us pull up a chair as the

BOOGIE WOOGIE BUGLE BOY

from BUCK PRIVATES

Words and Music by DON RAYE
and HUGHIE PRINCE

Medium Boogie Woogie

He was a fa-mous trum-pet man from out Chi-ca-go way, ___ He had a "boo-gie" style that no one else could play. ___ He was the top man of his craft

MCA Music Publishing

CALL ME IRRESPONSIBLE

from the Paramount Picture PAPA'S DELICATE CONDITION

Words by SAMMY CAHN
Music by JAMES VAN HEUSEN

CHANGE THE WORLD

featured on the Motion Picture Soundtrack PHENOMENON

Words and Music by GORDON KENNEDY,
WAYNE KIRKPATRICK and TOMMY SIMS

ba - by,_ if I_ could_ change _____

the _ world. ___ *Guitar solo*

Solo ends I could

CHIM CHIM CHER-EE
from Walt Disney's MARY POPPINS

Words and Music by RICHARD M. SHERMAN
and ROBERT B. SHERMAN

Tempo 1

CHINATOWN
from the Paramount Motion Picture CHINATOWN

Music by JERRY GOLDSMITH

COCKTAILS FOR TWO

from the Paramount Picture MURDER AT THE VANITIES

Words and Music by ARTHUR JOHNSTON
and SAM COSLOW

EXHALE (SHOOP SHOOP)
from the Original Soundtrack Album WAITING TO EXHALE

Words and Music by
BABYFACE

Easy R&B ballad

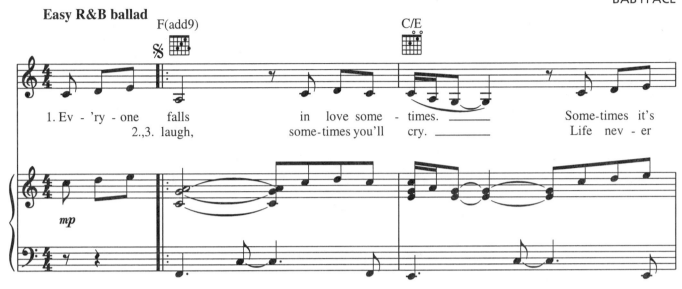

1. Ev - 'ry - one falls in love some - times. _____ Some-times it's
2.,3. laugh, some-times you'll cry. _____ Life nev - er

wrong _____ and some - times it's right. For ev - 'ry
tells _ us _____ the whens or whys. When you've got

win some - one must fail, but there comes a
friends to wish you well, you'll find a

DO YOU KNOW WHERE YOU'RE GOING TO?

Theme from MAHOGANY

Words by GERRY GOFFIN
Music by MIKE MASSER

THEME FROM E.T.
(The Extra-Terrestrial)
from the Universal Picture E.T. (THE EXTRA-TERRESTRIAL)

Music by
JOHN WILLIAMS

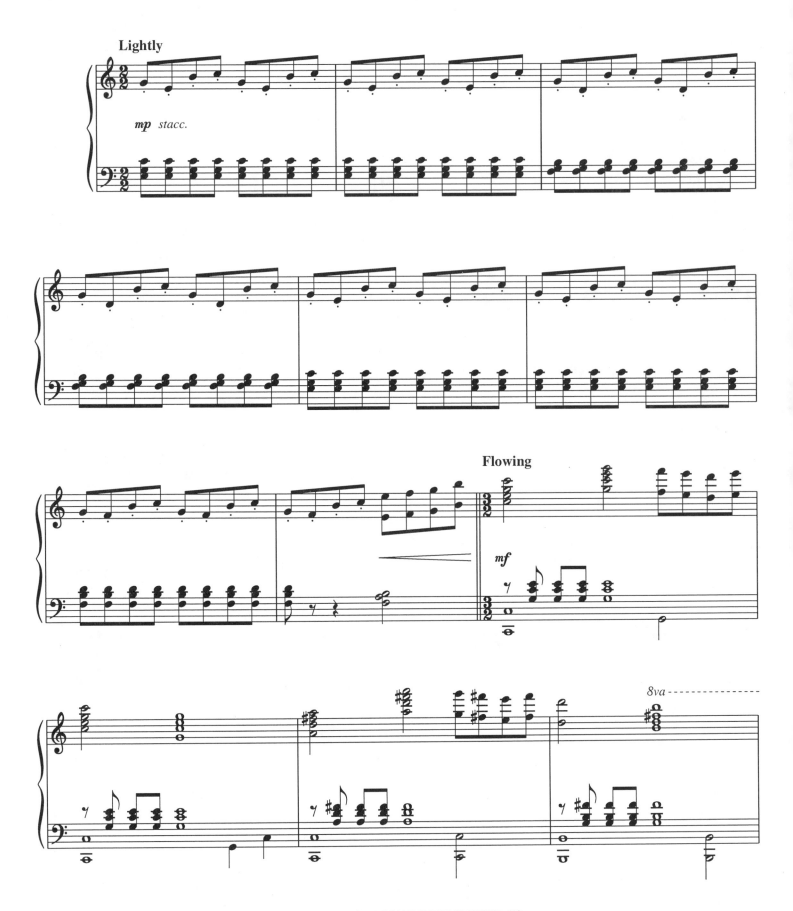

THE EXODUS SONG
from EXODUS

Words by PAT BOONE
Music by ERNEST GOLD

FLASHDANCE...WHAT A FEELING

from the Paramount Picture FLASHDANCE

Lyrics by KEITH FORSEY and IRENE CARA
Music by GIORGIO MORODER

THE GODFATHER
(Love Theme)
from the Paramount Picture THE GODFATHER

By NINO ROTA

Slowly and expressively

FORREST GUMP - MAIN TITLE
(Feather Theme)
from the Paramount Motion Picture FORREST GUMP

Music by ALAN SILVESTRI

(lightly)

GIGI
from GIGI

Words by ALAN JAY LERNER
Music by FREDERICK LOEWE

A GUY WHAT TAKES HIS TIME

from SHE DONE HIM WRONG

Words and Music by
RALPH RAINGER

I CONCENTRATE ON YOU
from BROADWAY MELODY OF 1940

Words and Music by
COLE PORTER

HELP!
from HELP!

Words and Music by JOHN LENNON
and PAUL McCARTNEY

I WISH I DIDN'T LOVE YOU SO

from the Paramount Picture THE PERILS OF PAULINE

Words and Music by
FRANK LOESSER

ISN'T IT ROMANTIC?

from the Paramount Picture LOVE ME TONIGHT

Words by LORENZ HART
Music by RICHARD RODGERS

(I've Had)
THE TIME OF MY LIFE
from DIRTY DANCING

Words and Music by FRANKE PREVITE,
JOHN DeNICOLA and DONALD MARKOWITZ

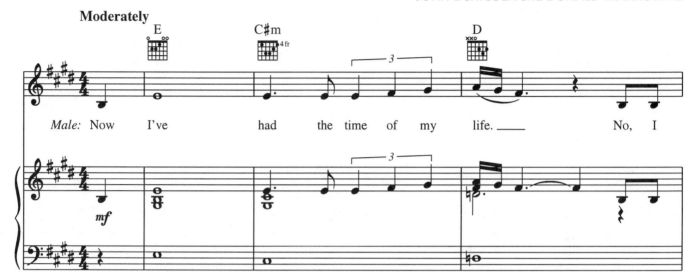

Male: Now I've had the time of my life. ___ No, I

nev - er felt ___ like this be - fore. Yes, I swear it's the truth, ___ and I

owe it all to you. ___
Female: 'Cause ___ I've had the time of my life, ___ and I

IF I HAD A TALKING PICTURE OF YOU

from SUNNY SIDE UP

Words and Music by RAY HENDERSON,
LEW BROWN and B.G. DeSYLVA

IN THE STILL OF THE NIGHT
from ROSALIE

Words and Music by
COLE PORTER

120

IT ALL DEPENDS ON YOU
from THE SINGING FOOL

Words and Music by B.G. DeSYLVA,
LEW BROWN and RAY HENDERSON

KOKOMO
from the Motion Picture COCKTAIL

Words and Music by MIKE LOVE, TERRY MELCHER,
JOHN PHILLIPS and SCOTT McKENZIE

Moderately bright

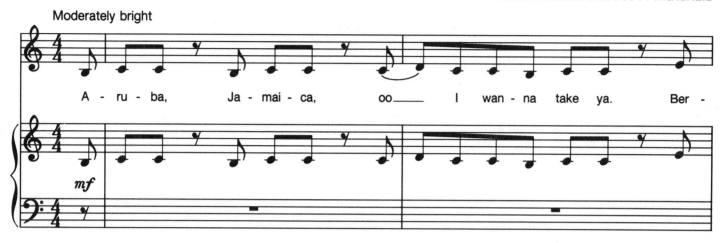

A - ru - ba, Ja - mai - ca, oo___ I wan - na take ya. Ber -

mu - da, Ba - ha - ma, come___ on, pret - ty ma - ma. Key Lar - go, Mon - te - go, Ba -

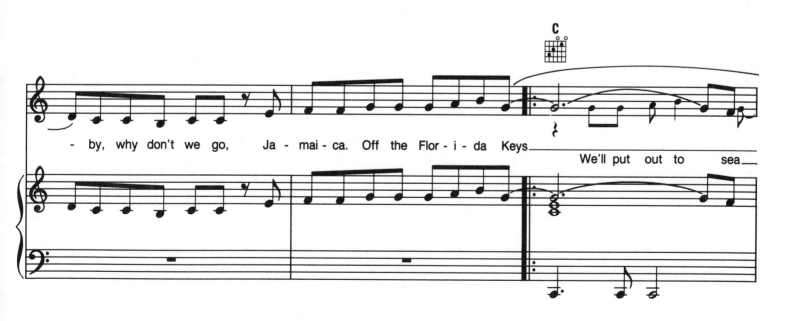

C

- by, why don't we go, Ja - mai - ca. Off the Flor - i - da Keys___ We'll put out to sea___

We'll be fall-ing in love____ to the rhy-thm of a
That dream-y look in your eye,____ give me a trop-i-cal

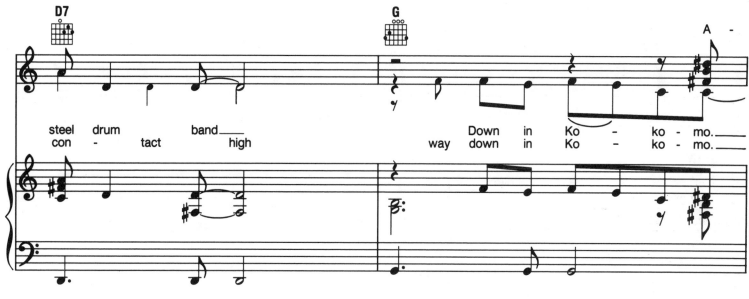

steel drum band____
con - tact band high

Down in Ko - ko - mo.____
way down in Ko - ko - mo.____

ru - ba

Ja - mai - ca, oo____ I wan-na take you to Ber -

mu - da, Ba - ha - ma. Come___ on, pret - ty ma - ma. Key

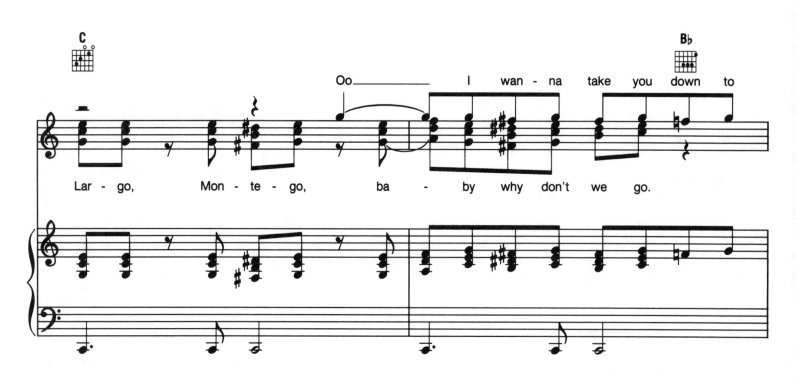

Lar - go, Mon - te - go, ba - by why don't we go.

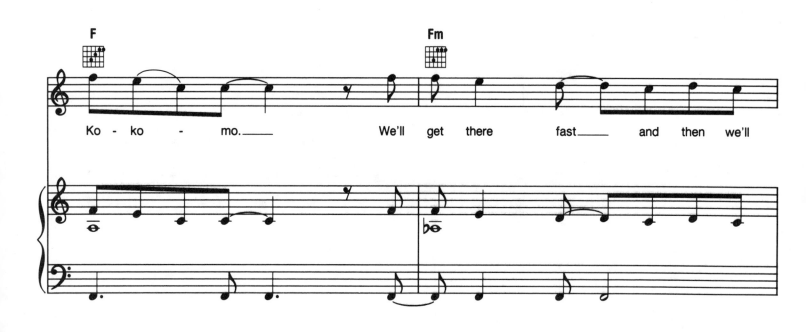

Ko - ko - mo.___ We'll get there fast___ and then we'll

IT MIGHT AS WELL BE SPRING

from STATE FAIR

Lyrics by OSCAR HAMMERSTEIN II
Music by RICHARD RODGERS

THE LADY'S IN LOVE WITH YOU
from the Paramount Picture SOME LIKE IT HOT

Words by FRANK LOESSER
Music by BURTON LANE

LAST DANCE
from THANK GOD IT'S FRIDAY

Words and Music by
PAUL JABARA

THEME FROM
"LAWRENCE OF ARABIA"
from LAWRENCE OF ARABIA

By MAURICE JARRE

THE LOOK OF LOVE
from CASINO ROYALE

Words by HAL DAVID
Music by BURT BACHARACH

LONG AGO
(And Far Away)
from COVER GIRL

Words by IRA GERSHWIN
Music by JEROME KERN

THE MAN THAT GOT AWAY
from the Motion Picture A STAR IS BORN

Lyric by IRA GERSHWIN
Music by HAROLD ARLEN

Slowly, but insistently

LOVE ME TENDER

from LOVE ME TENDER

Words and Music by ELVIS PRESLEY
and VERA MATSON

Love me ten-der, love me sweet,
Love me ten-der, love me long,
Love me ten-der, love me dear,
When at last my dreams come true,

nev - er let me go.
take me to your heart,
tell me you are mine.
dar - ling, this I know:

You have made my
for it's made there my
I'll be yours through
Hap - pi - ness will

LOVE STORY
Theme from the Paramount Picture LOVE STORY

Music by FRANCIS LAI

MAYBE THIS TIME
from the Musical CABARET

Words by FRED EBB
Music by JOHN KANDER

MONA LISA

from the Paramount Picture CAPTAIN CAREY, U.S.A.

Words and Music by JAY LIVINGSTON
and RAY EVANS

In a vil-la in a lit-tle old I-tal-ian town lives a girl whose beau-ty shames the rose. Man-y yearn to love her but their hopes all tum-ble down What does she want? No one knows! Mo-na

MOON RIVER
from the Paramount Picture BREAKFAST AT TIFFANY'S

Words by JOHNNY MERCER
Music by HENRY MANCINI

THE MUSIC OF GOODBYE
Love Theme from OUT OF AFRICA

Music by JOHN BARRY
Words by ALAN and MARILYN BERGMAN

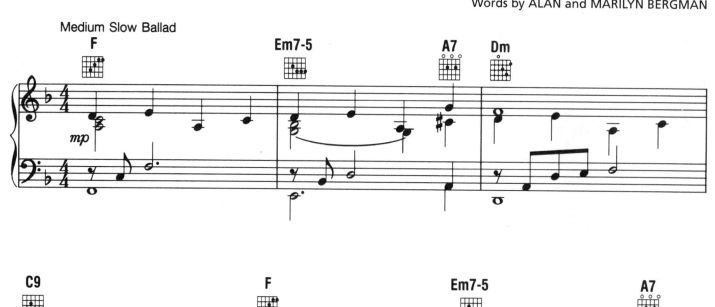

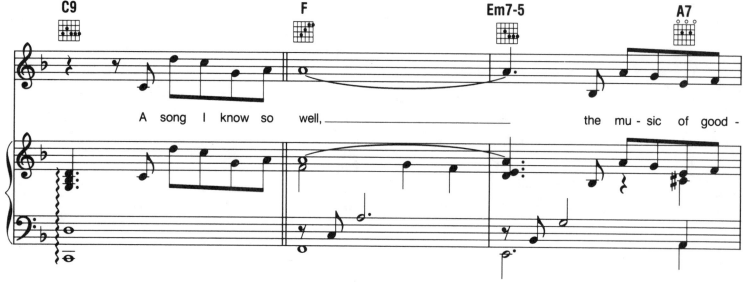

MY HEART WILL GO ON
(Love Theme from 'Titanic')
from the Paramount and Twentieth Century Fox Motion Picture TITANIC

Music by JAMES HORNER
Lyric by WILL JENNINGS

Ev - 'ry night in my dreams I see you, I

feel you, that is how I know you go on.

Once more you o - pen the door

and you're here in my heart, and my heart will go

To Coda

on and on.

Love can touch us one time and last for a

life - time, and nev-er let go till we're gone.

Love was when I loved you; one true time I

hold to. In my life we'll al - ways go on.

D.S. al Coda

CODA

on. _____

NO TWO PEOPLE
from the Motion Picture HANS CHRISTIAN ANDERSEN

By FRANK LOESSER

THE RAINBOW CONNECTION
from THE MUPPET MOVIE

By PAUL WILLIAMS
and KENNETH L. ASCHER

ONE FOR MY BABY
(And One More for the Road)
from the Motion Picture THE SKY'S THE LIMIT

Lyric by JOHNNY MERCER
Music by HAROLD ARLEN

PUTTIN' ON THE RITZ
from the Motion Picture PUTTIN' ON THE RITZ

Words and Music by
IRVING BERLIN

RAIDERS MARCH
from the Paramount Motion Picture RAIDERS OF THE LOST ARK

Music by JOHN WILLIAMS

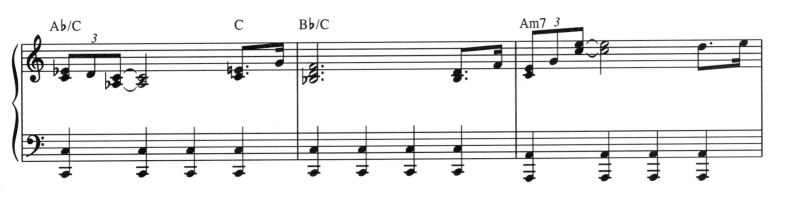

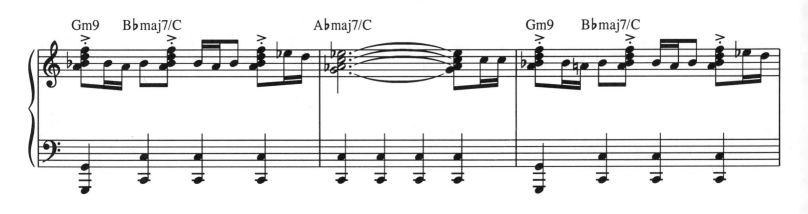

RAINDROPS KEEP FALLIN' ON MY HEAD

from BUTCH CASSIDY AND THE SUNDANCE KID

Lyric by HAL DAVID
Music by BURT BACHARACH

THE RIVER KWAI MARCH
from THE BRIDGE ON THE RIVER KWAI

By MALCOLM ARNOLD

March

ROMEO AND JULIET
(Love Theme)
from the Paramount Picture ROMEO AND JULIET

By NINO ROTA

STAYIN' ALIVE
from SATURDAY NIGHT FEVER

Words and Music by BARRY GIBB,
MAURICE GIBB and ROBIN GIBB

THEME FROM "SCHINDLER'S LIST"

from the Universal Motion Picture SCHINDLER'S LIST

Composed by JOHN WILLIAMS

SOMEWHERE IN TIME

from SOMEWHERE IN TIME

By JOHN BARRY

Moderately slow

SOMEWHERE, MY LOVE
Lara's Theme from DOCTOR ZHIVAGO

Lyric by PAUL FRANCIS WEBSTER
Music by MAURICE JARRE

SOONER OR LATER
(I Always Get My Man)
from the Film DICK TRACY

Words and Music by
STEPHEN SONDHEIM

Slow Swing, with a steady beat

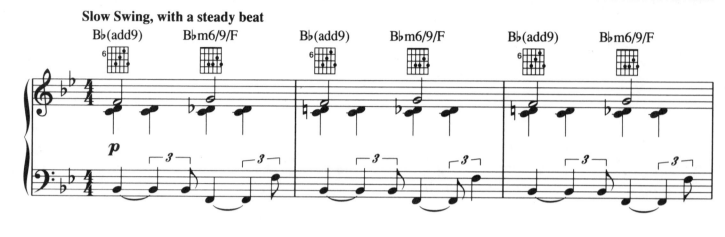

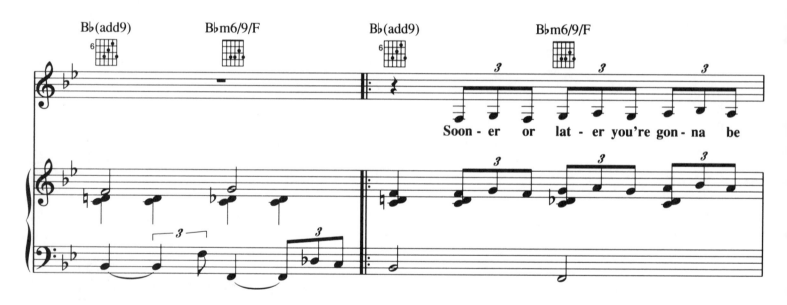

Soon-er or lat-er you're gon-na be

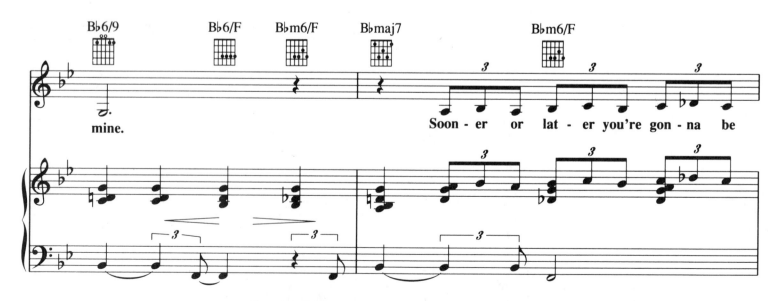

mine.   Soon-er or lat-er you're gon-na be

STEPPIN' OUT WITH MY BABY

from the Motion Picture Irving Berlin's EASTER PARADE

Words and Music by
IRVING BERLIN

SUMMERTIME IN VENICE
from the Motion Picture SUMMERTIME

English Words by CARL SIGMAN
Music by ICINI

MCA Music Publishing

TAKE MY BREATH AWAY
(Love Theme)
from the Paramount Picture TOP GUN

Words and Music by GIORGIO MORODER
and TOM WHITLOCK

Watch-ing ev-'ry mo-tion in ___
Watch-ing, I keep wait-ing, still ___
Watch-ing ev-'ry mo-tion in ___

___ my fool-ish lov-er's game; ___
___ an-tic-i-pat-ing love, ___
___ this fool-ish lov-er's game; ___

on this end-less o-cean, fi-
nev-er hes-i-tat-ing to ___
haunt-ed by the no-tion some-

TAXI DRIVER
(Theme)
from TAXI DRIVER

By BERNARD HERRMANN

Rubato, expressivo (slow feeling)

TEACHER'S PET

from TEACHER'S PET

Words and Music by
JOE LUBIN

TOO LATE NOW

from ROYAL WEDDING

Words by ALAN JAY LERNER
Music by BURTON LANE

THANKS FOR THE MEMORY

from the Paramount Picture BIG BROADCAST OF 1938

Words and Music by LEO ROBIN
and RALPH RAINGER

THAT OLD BLACK MAGIC

from the Paramount Picture STAR SPANGLED RHYTHM

Words by JOHNNY MERCER
Music by HAROLD ARLEN

THAT'S ENTERTAINMENT
from THE BAND WAGON

Words by HOWARD DIETZ
Music by ARTHUR SCHWARTZ

TOOT, TOOT, TOOTSIE!

(Good-Bye!)

from THE JAZZ SINGER

Words and Music by GUS KAHN,
ERNIE ERDMAN, DAN RUSSO and TED FIORITO

TOP HAT, WHITE TIE AND TAILS

from the RKO Radio Motion Picture TOP HAT

Words and Music by
IRVING BERLIN

Moderately

I just got an in-vi-ta-tion through the mails. _____ "Your pres-ence re-quest-ed this even-ing, it's for-mal." A top hat, a white tie and tails.

UNINVITED
from the Motion Picture CITY OF ANGELS

Words and Music by
ALANIS MORISSETTE

MCA Music Publishing

I don't think you un-wor - thy; I need a mo-ment to de-lib-er - ate. ___

Guitar solo ad lib.

Play 4 times

UNDER THE SEA
from Walt Disney's THE LITTLE MERMAID

Lyrics by HOWARD ASHMAN
Music by ALAN MENKEN

THE WAY WE WERE

from the Motion Picture THE WAY WE WERE

Words by ALAN and MARILYN BERGMAN
Music by MARVIN HAMLISCH

THE WAY YOU LOOK TONIGHT

from SWING TIME

Words by DOROTHY FIELDS
Music by JEROME KERN

A WHOLE NEW WORLD

from Walt Disney's ALADDIN

Music by ALAN MENKEN
Lyrics by TIM RICE

YES, YES!
from the Motion Picture PALMY DAYS

By CON CONRAD
and CLIFF FRIEND

I'm on my way, I'm on my way, I'm
I just can't wait, I just can't wait. Don't

YOU'LL BE IN MY HEART

(Pop Version)

from Walt Disney Pictures' TARZAN™

Words and Music by
PHIL COLLINS

Come stop your cry - ing; it will be all right.

Just take my hand, hold it tight. I will pro - tect you from

all a - round you. I will be here; don't you cry.

ZIP-A-DEE-DOO-DAH
from Walt Disney's SONG OF THE SOUTH

Words by RAY GILBERT
Music by ALLIE WRUBEL

Additional Lyrics

2. Zip-a-dee-doo-dah, Zip-a-dee-ay,
My, oh my, what a wonderful day.
Plenty of sunshine headin' our way.
We never doubted he'd get away.
Movin' on taught him a lesson,
You learned it well Brer Rabbit,
Getting caught's a nasty habit.
Zip-a-dee-doo-dah, zip-a-dee-ay
  wonderful feeling, feeling this way.
  (To Bridge)

3. Zip-a-dee-doo-dah, Zip-a-dee-ay,
Brer Fox and Brer Bear gonna get it today.
Zip-a-dee-doo-dah, Zip-a-dee-ay,
That hungry gator's getting his way,
Mister Bluebird on my shoulder
It's the truth it's actual
Everything is satisfactual.
Zip-a-dee-doo-dah, Zip-a-dee-ay,
Wonderful feeling, wonderful day.